Precipitation                12.95

Author:            Sievert, Terri
Reading Level:  3.7
Point Value:     0.5
Quiz Number:    84627

Accelerated Reader

D1606901

Weather Update

# Precipitation

by Terri Sievert

**Consultant:**
Joseph M. Moran, PhD
Associate Director, Education Program
American Meteorological Society, Washington, D.C.

Mankato, Minnesota

Bridgestone Books are published by Capstone Press,
151 Good Counsel Drive, P.O. Box 669, Mankato, Minnesota 56002.
www.capstonepress.com

*Library of Congress Cataloging-in-Publication Data*
Sievert, Terri.
    Precipitation / by Terri Sievert.
    p. cm.—(Bridgestone books. Weather update)
    Includes bibliographical references and index.
    ISBN 0-7368-3737-X (hardcover)
    1. Precipitation (Meteorology)—Juvenile literature. 2. Rain and rainfall—Juvenile literature. 3. Snow—Juvenile literature.  I. Title. II. Series.
QC924.7.S54 2005
551.57'7—dc22                                                                          2004010845

Summary: Discusses the different forms of precipitation and how rain and snow are measured.

**Editorial Credits**
Christopher Harbo, editor; Molly Nei, set designer; Wanda Winch, photo researcher;
    Scott Thoms, photo editor

**Photo Credits**
Bruce Coleman Inc./John H. Hoffman, 12; Roy Morsch, 6
Comstock, 1
Corbis/Charles O'Rear, 4; Richard Hutchings, 8; Royalty-Free, 18 (snow and tree)
Dan Delaney Photography, cover (child), back cover
Folio Inc./Michael Ventura, 14
Photodisc/C Squared Studios, 18 (ruler); Dan Farrall, cover (background)
Richard Hamilton Smith, 10
Tom Pantages, 16, 20

1 2 3 4 5 6 10 09 08 07 06 05

# Table of Contents

Condensation

Evaporation

Precipitation

# What Is Precipitation?

Rain makes puddles on the sidewalk. Snowflakes drift into piles on the ground. Rain and snow are made of water. They are forms of precipitation.

Precipitation is part of the water cycle. Water **evaporates** from lakes and oceans. It rises into the air as **water vapor**.

Water vapor cools and **condenses** as it rises. It forms droplets or ice crystals. Millions of tiny droplets or ice crystals form a cloud. The droplets or ice crystals grow larger. They fall to the ground as precipitation.

◄ The water cycle uses evaporation, condensation, and precipitation to move water from place to place.

# Rain

Raindrops form inside clouds. Water vapor condenses on tiny pieces of dust. A tiny water droplet forms. Wind blows the water droplet. The droplet hits smaller droplets and grows larger. The droplet becomes a raindrop and falls to the ground.

Raindrops can also begin as ice crystals. The ice crystals grow into snowflakes high in the clouds. Warm air melts the snowflakes as they fall from the clouds. They reach the ground as raindrops.

◀ A gentle rain brings flowers the water they need to live and grow.

# Snow

Snowflakes form inside clouds. Water vapor forms an ice crystal. Wind carries the ice crystal through the cloud. It strikes **supercooled** water droplets. The droplets freeze on the crystal. The ice crystal grows into a snowflake.

Snowflakes form at 32 degrees Fahrenheit (0 degrees Celsius) or colder. Snowflakes that form near this temperature look flat. They have six sides. Snowflakes that form between 25 and 21 degrees Fahrenheit (minus 4 and minus 6 degrees Celsius) look like needles.

◄ A winter storm blankets the ground and trees with snow and makes everything look white.

# Sleet

Sleet begins as snowflakes. The snowflakes fall into warmer air and melt into raindrops. The raindrops fall from the warm air into cold air. They freeze into small pieces of ice.

Sleet bounces when it hits the ground. It does not stick to things. You can hear it hit windows and rooftops.

Sleet often falls in autumn when air temperatures are growing colder.

# Hail

Hail forms when ice particles in a thunderstorm run into supercooled water droplets. Many layers of ice build up on the ice particles. Hail falls to the ground when it is too heavy for air currents to hold it up.

Hail can damage many things. It dents cars, damages roofs, and breaks windows. Hail also ruins crops. It strips away leaves and cuts down plants. Large hailstones can even hurt people.

◄ Marble-sized hail falls on a country road during a thunderstorm.

# Freezing Rain

Ice storms bring freezing rain. Most freezing rain starts as snow. The snow melts into rain as it falls. The raindrops fall through a layer of freezing air near the ground. The raindrops become supercooled.

When the raindrops hit cold objects on the ground, they turn to ice. Freezing rain coats everything it touches in ice.

Ice storms can be dangerous. Cars skid off roads covered with ice. People slip on icy sidewalks. A heavy coating of ice can break tree limbs and bring down power lines.

◀ An ice storm leaves behind a heavy layer of ice that breaks power lines and tree branches.

funnel

tube →

← scale

# Measuring Rainfall

Rain is measured with a rain **gauge**. Some rain gauges use a **funnel** to catch raindrops. A scale shows how much rain has fallen in inches or centimeters.

A funnel rain gauge sits inside a large tube. In a big storm, rain fills up the funnel. Extra water collects inside the tube. The water in the funnel is measured first. The rain in the tube is measured next. The two amounts are added together to get the total rainfall.

◄ A rain gauge has a scale on the side of its funnel that measures rainfall.

18

# Measuring Snowfall

Snow is measured with a ruler. A flat surface is cleaned before a snowstorm. The snow falls on the surface. A ruler is placed in the snow. The ruler shows how many inches or centimeters of snow fell.

Sometimes snow is melted and the water left behind is measured. The snow falls into a tube and melts. A scale on the tube shows how much water was in the snow. About 10 inches (25 centimeters) of snow melt down to 1 inch (2.5 centimeters) of water.

◄ A ruler shows the snow is more than 13 inches (33 centimeters) deep.

# Forecasting Precipitation

Weather forecasters predict precipitation by studying **satellite** pictures and **radar** images. Satellites in space take pictures of clouds. Radar stations on the ground show where rain or snow is falling.

Forecasters also check air temperatures when precipitation is coming. Rain falls when temperatures are above freezing. Snow falls when temperatures are below freezing.

Forecasters try to tell when precipitation will fall. How cold is it today? Do you think you might see rain or snow?

◀ A weather forecaster studies a radar picture to predict where rain will fall.

# Glossary

condense (kuhn-DENSS)—to turn from a gas into a liquid

evaporate (i-VAP-uh-rate)—to change from a liquid into
 a gas

funnel (FUHN-uhl)—an open cone that narrows to
 a tube

gauge (GAYJ)—an instrument used for measuring

radar (RAY-dar)—an instrument that uses microwaves to
 locate precipitation

satellite (SAT-uh-lite)—a spacecraft that circles earth; satellites
 take pictures of clouds and storms.

supercooled (SOO-pur-koold)—to be cooled below the freezing
 point without turning into a solid

water vapor (WAW-tur VAY-pur)—water in gas form; water
 vapor is one of the many invisible gases in air.

# Read More

**Rodgers, Alan, and Angella Streluk.** *Precipitation.*
Measuring the Weather. Chicago: Heinemann, 2003.

**Trueit, Trudi Strain.** *Rain, Hail, and Snow.* Watts Library.
New York: Franklin Watts, 2002.

# Internet Sites

FactHound offers a safe, fun way to find
Internet sites related to this book. All of
the sites on FactHound have been
researched by our staff.

Here's how:
1. Visit *www.facthound.com*
2. Type in this special code **073683737X** for
   age-appropriate sites. Or enter a search word
   related to this book for a more general search.
3. Click on the **Fetch It** button.

FactHound will fetch the best sites for you!

# Index

GAYLORD M